True and Faithful Friends

Smokey Culver

True and Faithful Friends
© 2019 Smokey Culver

ISBN: 978-1-970003-46-8

Cover Artwork © Red Dashboard LLC
Cover Design © Frankie Lopez, Jr.

Published by
Red Dashboard LLC Publishing
Princeton NJ 08540
www.reddashboard.com

More Books
by Smokey Culver

A Wrap and a Hooey
Cowboy Poetry

Ridin' Shotgun
Cowboy Poetry

Available on Amazon and in the
RedDashboard.com Catalog

For Jenny...

I guess a passion for animals runs in my family. My daughter, Jenny, has shown so much kindness and care for animals of all kinds, and in the past few years has rescued, fostered, and found homes for countless puppies of all ages and breeds. It takes a special kind of person to devote this much time and energy to rescuing God's 4-legged (and in some cases 3-legged) creatures, spending hours on end with her friends at Second Chance Pets, helping find forever homes for rescued fur babies. And much like it has been for me with the horses, she has nursed many a sick puppy that just didn't survive. But rather than giving in to the sadness and walking away, she continues to take on each challenge that comes her way.

To say I am proud of Jenny would be quite an understatement. I dedicate this book to my awesome daughter. Thanks for all you do!

Table of Contents

A Moment with a True and Faithful Friend 1
One Last Ride with My Buddy 3
Chained 5
Cowboys Never Cry 7
Mutts 9
Dogs Don't Care 11
In Memoriam: Over The Rainbow Bridge 13
Pasture Pals 15
Shelter Dogs 17
He Will Run to the Arms of His Friend 19
That Old Dog 21
Farewell Baby Hollis 23
Rope You a Good 'Un 25
My Palomino Lady 27
Stepping High and Proud 29
You Called Her Baby 31
Our Paco 34
No More Wheels for Odin 36

A Moment with a True and Faithful Friend

Old friend, I'm glad to see
      your tail still waggin' like it is
Your happiness just rubs
      right off on me
And I love every moment
      that we sit out in the yard
Just like before,
      beneath our favorite tree
I think of when I brought you home
      so many years ago
You knew that this was
      where you're meant to be
And from that day you stayed beside me,
      never far away
Your job in life
      was just protecting me
We've seen a lot of good times,
      and some bad ones, you and I
You seem to know
      when I am feeling down
That little nudge you give me
      just to show me you are here
It means so much
      just having you around
So, as we spend a little time to reminisce a bit
      and I reach out to touch you once again
I realize how much they mean,
      these visits that we have
A moment with a true and faithful friend

1

You look at me so lovingly
        each time that you appear
And leave your friends
        where they will run and play
You hang with me a little while
        until it's time to go
Back to the Rainbow Bridge so far away...

One Last Ride with My Buddy

It's been awhile since he's been gone,
and life goes on, they say
But I still miss that dog so much,
it feels like yesterday
Our years together, how they flew,
but so it is, I guess
I tried to see that every day
we shared would be the best
And when I saw the signs that he
was not so well, I tried
To act if he was OK,
yet knew it was a lie
The doctors said just care for him
as long as he could stand
And when the time did come,
we'd go ahead with things as planned
I couldn't bear to watch my buddy
 when the pain was such
That he cried out each time I reached
to give a gentle touch
I guess of all the years I've lived
that was my hardest day
To make the call to let them know
that we were on our way
We sat together in the back seat
traveling side by side
With thoughts of what was coming,
it was such a painful ride
I told him all along the way

that it would be okay
While knowing in my heart that
this would be our final day
We put him on the table
as he looked at me with trust
I stared into his eyes and said,
"I Love you very much"
I watched him take his final breath;
I cried as he moved on
I had to face the fact that
my old pal was really gone
And now the time has passed,
and I can think of him again
Recalling all his antics while
reflecting with a grin
And when I sit with coffee
underneath our favorite tree
I feel my buddy's presence
with his paw upon my knee...

Chained

His ears perk up each time
        he sees somebody walk his way
His tail is wagging now
         because he knows
He's going to have a visitor,
        he shifts from paw to paw
'Cause someone's taking time to say hello

The highlight of a puppy's day
        when tied up to a tree
When his whole world's
        a 4-foot piece of chain
Is having someone
        show a bit of kindness, pat his head
And let him know you understand his pain

He spends his days and nights
        right where you see him, never moves
He never gets to run
        and chase a ball
He'll never chase a rabbit
        out across an open field
Nor have that opportunity at all

Yes, he gets food and water,
        even got a little shed
To get out of the weather
        when it rains

5

Now doesn't he deserve a better life
        than what he has?
Though even if he could,
        he'd not complain

A dog is born with loyalty,
        he doesn't hold a grudge
And if he's treated badly
        he forgives
But why can't people see
        the torment in that puppy's eyes
And understand this is no way to live...?

Cowboys Never Cry

He showed up at the rescue
and it brought you to your knees
to see how much that pony had endured

A life of more neglect
than any animal should know
and sadly, healing never is assured

He's down, you called the vet,
you know his time is running out
you gotta help him get up on his feet

He throws his head back,
tries to plant his front ones on the ground
with all your efforts ending in defeat

The needle is the last resort,
you pray that he'll pull through
his eyes are telling you he wants to live

And your job is to help him,
you will save him if you can
you're going to give it all you have to give

But it was just not meant to be,
the doc has made the call
his breathing grows more shallow as he lies

Upon the cold wet ground, he twitches,
takes his final breath
while you stand back and sadly watch him die

You pull your hat brim lower
as you look down at him there
you don't want anyone to see your eyes

Cause that must be arena sand
that blew up in your face
and we all know that cowboys never cry...

Mutts

They come in every color,
        every size and every shape
They're every bit as loyal
        and as true
As any dog with miles of pedigree
        behind their name
And all they want
        is just to be with you
I'm talkin' 'bout that silly mutt
        with big old floppy ears
The one that jumps with joy
        each time you meet
And you don't care that he's a mix
        of many doggy breeds
Because his place in life
        is at your feet
He may not have a wall of trophies
        for the best in show
He may not look
        as stately as the ones
Who prance around the ring
        and hold their head up in the air
But chasing sticks,
        for him is lots of fun
And he'll be your companion
        till the day he leaves this world
His place will be beside you
        till the end

He asks for nothing in return,
        you're everything he needs
He's surely earned the title
        Man's Best Friend
So, when you look down at him,
        you just know that he's the best
That ever sniffed
        another doggie's butt
He's happy as can be
        just knowing that he is your pal
None other like 'em;
        gotta love them mutts...

Dogs Don't Care

Dogs don't care how rich you are,
they don't care what you drive
and they don't care if you are fat or thin

You know they never need you to be
someone you are not
they don't care where you're going or where you've been

And wouldn't this old world just be
a whole lot better place
if people looked at things the way dogs do

With only love and trust
for those that show a little sign
of kindness, with a heart that is so true

And even when they're treated badly,
they forgive so fast
a kind word and a friendly little pat

They never hold a grudge,
they never wish you any harm
I only wish that I could be like that

When God made dogs for man's best friend,
He made them very well
and when he did, He left off any flaws

He taught them how to make our cares
and worries go away
by reaching out to touch us with a paw

It doesn't take a lot to make
a dog feel really loved
the slightest touch assures your love is there

And in return you get to be
the center of their world
no matter who you are 'cause dogs don't care...

In Memoriam: Over The Rainbow Bridge

Just this side of heaven is a place called Rainbow Bridge. When an animal dies that has been especially close to someone here, that pet goes to Rainbow Bridge. There are meadows and hills for all of our special friends, so they can run and play together.

Pasture Pals

Ya know, it's really something,
        that connection that they have
They never seem to
        wander very far
They spend each day together,
        you see one you see them both
And I guess pasture pals
        is what they are
I wonder what they're thinking
        and if they communicate
When they spend every moment
        side by side
And one gets so upset
        when they get left behind because
Their buddy has been taken for a ride
This seems to be a friendship
        with unspoken dialog
Two equines share their feelings in their way
Like folks who spend an evening, dinner,
        wine and candle light
They have their time together munching hay
I wonder if they gossip
        'bout the others in the herd
Or laugh on frosty mornings
        when they run
I wonder if they like the winter blankets
        that they wear
Or gripe about the hot
        South Texas sun

I guess I'll never know
        just what goes on between these two
No, all that I can do is speculate
And if they're talkin' 'bout me,
        well I hope their words are kind
These pasture pals
        are really pretty great...

Shelter Dogs

They spend their days and nights
      inside a chain link prison cell
These shelter dogs,
      they sadly must endure
A life of never knowing what tomorrow's
      going to bring
From day to day
      their destiny unsure
Some shiver in the corner,
      what a sad sight to behold
They've never felt a soft and gentle touch
While there are those
      that jump for joy when someone says hello
A word of kindness
      means so very much
What stories they could tell of what they've seen
      and where they've been
You look into their eyes
      and you can see
The sadness and the anguish
      as you pass them one by one
As they sincerely make their silent plea
Today may be the day for him
      to leave this noisy place
He watches as they open up the gate
He sees the leash, he hears the words,
      "Come on, it's time to go!"
He shifts from paw to paw,
      he cannot wait

The others sadly watch
      as they know they must stay behind
But then tomorrow is another day
As every day that passes
      brings them closer to their fate
May they all find forever homes, I pray...

He Will Run to the Arms of His Friend

It's such a sad day
        when we must say farewell
to a pet
        that we've had for so long
And we dream of the day
        when we'll see him again
and our love
        will remain ever strong

But what of the one
        who has been left behind
when his master
         has met his reward
And there's no way to tell him,
        no way to explain
as he patiently waits
        in the yard

Days pass
        and someone adopts him at last
and in a new home
        he will dwell
Though confused
        he just can't understand what went wrong
yet he's cared for
        and treated so well

As he sits waiting
       patiently knowing his friend
will certainly come
       back today
Another day passes,
       then two and then three
and he feels
       as if he's been betrayed

There's no way he'd know it
       but when their time comes
to that great Rainbow Bridge,
       he'll ascend
He will hear a familiar voice
       calling his name
And he'll run to the
       arms of his friend…

That Old Dog

That old dog wasn't your idea of a pet
When you glanced at his cloudy old eyes
And you saw all the gray in his face as he met you
So happy because you stopped by
That old dog just wasn't what you had in mind
When you set out to bring home a pup
But you gave him a chance and he's now your best friend
He's a blessing you didn't pass up
He may not be around for the next 15 years
But for what time is left, you can bet
He'll be your companion, he'll stay by your side
And what more could you ask of a pet
Though he can't run to meet you on feeble old legs
When you come home from work every day
He stands waiting patiently till you arrive
Wagging tail with his muzzle of gray
He'll have no fear of dying when his days are done
And he'll trust you to know when it's time
And he'll look in your eyes as he takes his last breath
And he'll know it's the end of the line
But he won't share your sadness when you
shed those tears
'Cause he's had some good years as your friend
And he'll make his way on to that great Rainbow Bridge
Where he'll wait till he sees you again...

"Baby Hollis"

Farewell Baby Hollis

So long little buddy,
  it's hard to believe
That your time with us
  came to an end
But your spirit
  has lifted our own for awhile
And you had made
  so many friends
In the time that we knew you,
  you struggled along
As you faced every day
  that you had
With courage and bravery,
  you never gave up
And your passing
  has left us so sad
There is no guarantee
  that tomorrow is ours
And we only have
  what we can see
But our little friend Hollis,
  you showed us the way
To embrace every day
  we receive
There's a place where
  our donkeys and horses will wait
At the end
  of that bridge in a field

Where you'll run with your friends
        through the meadows above
And you'll play
        and you'll kick up your heels
But we'll miss you a lot
        and we'll never forget
Those big ears
        and that look in your eyes
So, take care little friend,
        and look down now and then
Till we see you in Heaven, good-bye...

Rope You a Good 'Un

Rope you a good 'un in the ol' horse corral
Get a pony that's steady and strong
Got a whole lot of pasture to ride 'fore you're done
And the day, well it's gonna be long
He may buck just a little, on this cold winter morn'
He's just sayin' he's feelin' his oats
So, before you mount up, better tighten that cinch
Pull your hat down and button your coat
If you're chasin' a wild one, and wild they can be
Those cattle will duck and they'll hide
That pony will track an ol' cow through the brush
While you just hang on for the ride
A partnership 'tween a cowboy and horse
I'll tell you, it ain't nothin' new
There's an unspoken language, a touch of the reins
And a horse's response to the cue
You may not know his name,
and he sure don't know yours
But like you he just knows what to do
He's your partner from sunup till day's work is done
You're a team, that ol' pony and you
So, when the day's over, the cows are all penned
And you've covered a few miles of sod
Just give that ol' pony a pat on the rump
and he'll know that he did a good job...

Palomino "Lady"

My Palomino Lady

Old but she was gentle,
      seems we made a perfect match
That palomino mare
      I had back then
I was pretty little
      at eleven years of age
So, Lady
      was my perfect equine friend
A big one standing 16 hands,
      with main and tail of white
I thought she was
      the finest of her kind
So gentle and
      so patient as we piled on one by one
She took us down the road
      a thousand times
I learned a lot from caring
      for a horse back in those years
I rode my bike
      a pretty darn good ways
Out to Golden Acres
      where my Lady gal would wait
I brushed her, fed her,
      cared for her each day
And on the nights the rodeo
      was happenin' down the road
I'd saddle up
      and head out all alone

My Lady took me there and back,
        she never missed a step
She never failed
        to get me safely home
I've had a lot of horses
        since those days so long ago
When Lady was
        my noble trusty mare
But I just have a feeling
        when I head for my reward
My Lady is the one
        who'll greet me there...

Stepping High and Proud

You got to see a miracle
the day that he was born
And something told you he was going to be

Not only your first horse, but your companion,
your best friend
And to your heart, he'd always hold the key

At 16 years, you brought him
from his Colorado home
To be with you down south, and you were blessed

As time went by you came
to love this noble equine mount
There was no question, Target was the best

You never had to worry
if you let somebody ride
Cause he was such a calm and gentle soul

He greeted everyone the same,
you never were surprised
But that was Target; that was how he rolled

Now, if you had a swig or two
of beer that you could spare
He'd throw one back without a second thought

Then there were the cigarettes,
he'd sneak a pack for sure
And he would eat them if he wasn't caught

Your years together, Target was your soul mate to the end
Parades and trail rides, what a team you were!
And losing him, it was the hardest thing you've ever done
And anyone who knows you will concur

But there's a place we hear about,
a field of emerald green
Your Target will be waiting till the day

He'll look across the meadow
and perk up his ears because
He'll see you coming as you run his way

Once again you'll swing up
in the saddle and he'll prance
This awesome creature, stepping high and proud

He'll hold his head up high
as equine angels step aside
When you and Target ride into the clouds...

You Called Her Baby

You've owned a lot of horses,
really good ones through the years
But then one day, you met a certain bay

And there was something special,
something in the Master Plan
She'd be the one to steal your heart away

In halter competitions,
she stood out among the best
And she was born with cow sense, what a mare!

An all-around fine pony,
great with little folks as well
The two of you were such an awesome pair

She loved to get a bath
and gobble down those ginger snaps
though somewhat stubborn if the truth be told

You think of how the friendship grew,
a bond meant to be
Those memories now are worth their weight in gold

Our time here in this earthly world
is never guaranteed
And yes, we wish we'd never have to part

We cherish every moment
till we have to let them go
With teary eyes, and yes, a broken heart

But there's an emerald meadow
where the crystal water flows
Where angel horses fly in easy gait

A bridge of rainbow colors,
where you'll gaze through happy tears
That special place in Heaven where they wait

You'll see so many horses
coming up to greet you there
You'll recognize them all, by style and breed

But one will not be taking
second place in line this time
This time you'll see your Baby in the lead…

Our Paco

The Habitat for Horses is a special kind of place
Our guests who come here get a second chance
And Paco is our self-appointed barnyard CEO
You'll know this little donkey at a glance
If donkeys had a way of smiling, he would surely grin
When anyone takes time to scratch his ears
He's got the most seniority of any in the herd
He's been around the ranch a lot of years
And when we have a pizza party for the working crew
On springtime days when weather's really nice
Don't turn your back 'cause if you do
you're in for a surprise
Ol' Paco's surely gonna sneak a slice
While equines have a tendency to pair up with a friend
And hang around together every day
Our Paco doesn't fit that mold it seems he needs his space
'Cause Paco is a loner all the way
Our little donkey mostly white with markings of a paint
And ears that stand up pointed to the sky
He's always glad to see you and he'll steal your heart away
Our Paco, he is just that kind of guy...

No More Wheels for Odin

~A Very Special Rott-Wheeler~

He wasn't like the other dogs,
       though he had not a clue
That he was handicapped,
       no not at all
Our Odin was just happy
       to be Odin, what a boy
Like any dog who loves
       to chase a ball
As handsome as a dog could be,
       his coat how it did shine
Those loving eyes would steal
       your heart away
A blessing to the ones
       who got to know this Rottie boy
A hero right up
       through his final day
Now there was something different
       'bout our Odin, you should know
A feature that he
       could not keep concealed
While other dogs all ran around
       and played on their 4 legs
Our Odin was a doggie
       who had wheels!
This really didn't bother him,
       'cause dogs don't seem to care

If they don't look
        just like the others do
Heck, he was just as happy
        rollin' round and making friends
As any other pup
        you ever knew
Now he has left us for his home
        where doggies wait above
And in this place,
        he will not be confined
He'll jump and play
        until the day he greets us at the Bridge
'Cause when he went,
        he left his wheels behind

Smokey Culver
Poet Laureate of Pasadena, Texas

- Born- August 4, 1949
- Grew up – Pasadena, TX
- Team Roper, Calf Roper, Farrier
- Union Pacific Railroad 1970-1995
- Railroad Safety Consultant 1995-present
- Ranch Hand and Investigator at Habitat for Horses Rescue Ranch in Galveston County, TX
- Performer at George Ranch Historical Park, Roping Demonstrations
- Featured Cowboy Poetry Columnist, Poolville Post (TX)
- Guest Poet on Various Radio and TV Shows
- 2018 Designated Poet Laureate of Pasadena, Texas
- "What Makes a Man a Cowboy?" Finalist NFR Cowboy Poetry Contest Las Vegas 2014
- Poet of the Year 2013, Texas Independence Day Celebration at the Courthouse in Granbury, TX
- Memberships: Academy of Western Artists; Western Music Association; Western Music Association, TX; San Jacinto Poets Society of TX

"I write about whatever comes to mind, mostly farmers and ranchers and down-home folks, and the rural/western way of life. The Lord has blessed me with an ability to put thoughts into words that generally make sense, and even stir up emotions sometimes. My poems are both happy and sad. If I make you laugh, I have done my job. If I make you cry, I have done my job."

Made in the USA
Middletown, DE
30 April 2022

64951007R00031